PANCAKES
FOR
BREAKFAST

PANCAKES
FOR
BREAKFAST

BY

TOMIE dePAOLA

HARCOURT BRACE & COMPANY
Orlando   Atlanta   Austin   Boston   San Francisco   Chicago   Dallas   New York
Toronto   London

FOR BETTY CAVE ♡

This edition is published by special arrangement with Harcourt Brace & Company.

Pancakes For Breakfast by Tomie dePaola. Copyright © 1978 by Tomie dePaola and Harcourt Brace & Company. Reprinted by permission of Harcourt Brace & Company.

Printed in the United States of America

ISBN 0-15-302100-4

3 4 5 6 7 8 9 10   035   97 96 95 94